We are the UNITED STATES

ACTIVITY BOOK

WIDE EYED EDITIONS

Say hello to the people of the USA!

You are about to take a tour of the people and cultures that call the United States of America home. As you complete the activities in this book, you'll discover the vibrant communities, regional traditions, and extraordinary places that make up this wonderful country.

LET'S GET STARTED!

WASHINGTON

MONTANA

NORTH DAKOTA

OREGON

IDAHO

SOUTH DAKOTA

WYOMING

NEBRASKA

NEVADA

UTAH

COLORADO

KANSAS

CALIFORNIA

OKLAHOMA

ARIZONA

NEW MEXICO

TEXAS

Turn to the **BACK** of the book for the answers to all of the puzzles.

This map shows all the states in the mainland US.

Can you color the map using only **four colors**, so that no two states that share a border are the same color?

MINNESOTA

VERMONT

MAINE

WISCONSIN

NEW YORK

NEW HAMPSHIRE

MICHIGAN

IOWA

PENNSYLVANIA

MASSACHUSETTS

OHIO

RHODE ISLAND

ILLINOIS

INDIANA

WEST VIRGINIA

CONNECTICUT

MISSOURI

KENTUCKY

VIRGINIA

NEW JERSEY

NORTH CAROLINA

DELAWARE

TENNESSEE

MARYLAND

ARKANSAS

SOUTH CAROLINA

WASHINGTON, D.C.

GEORGIA

ALABAMA

MISSISSIPPI

FLORIDA

LOUISIANA

Tip: Write each color in the state before coloring it in, so you know it will work.

Who's Who?

The US has been home to inspiring activists, creative musicians and writers, superstar sportspeople, brainy scientists, and more amazing people.

One person in this gallery was born in Acoma Pueblo, the oldest continuously occupied place in the US. Using the clues opposite, can you figure out who they are?

Look at the pictures and read the facts about each person. Cross out the people who don't match the clues, then circle the one who remains.

KATHERINE JOHNSON
1918–2020
Mathematician at NASA who helped send astronauts to the Moon.

ANN BANCROFT
B. 1955
First woman in history to cross the ice to the North Pole.

BARACK OBAMA
B. 1961
First Black president of the US.

SAM BERNS
1996–2014
Activist who raised awareness of progeria, the rare condition he was born with.

MADAM C.J. WALKER
1867–1919
Entrepreneur who created hair products for Black people.

DAVID MILLS
B. 1938
Programmer who helped develop the Internet.

JEANETTE RANKIN
1880–1973
First woman elected to the US Congress, in 1916.

MOSES "BLACK" HARRIS
? –1849
Famed mountain man, explorer, and guide on the Oregon Trail.

DOLLY PARTON
B. 1946
Country music artist, actor, businesswoman, and humanitarian.

MARGARET MURIE
1902–2003
Naturalist who campaigned for wildlife protection.

PRINCESS RED WING
1896–1987
Narragansett and Wampanoag activist.

THOMAS GARRETT
1789–1871
A leader of the Underground Railroad, which freed hundreds of enslaved people.

Say Hello!

Did you know that the US doesn't have an official language?
Most people speak English, but hundreds of other languages are also spoken.

The people below are saying "**hello**" in different languages.
To find out what they are, you'll need to crack the codes!

A	B	C	D	E	F	G	H	I	J	K	L	M	N	O	P	Q	R	S	T	U	V	W	X	Y	Z
26		24		21								16					11							4	1

YA'AT'EEH
13 26 5 26 17 12

HOLA
8 11 26 13 18 8 19

ALOHA
19 26 4 26 18 18 26 13

SALAM
26 9 26 25 18 24

NAMASTE
19 18 13 23 18

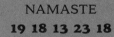

E NLE O
2 12 9 6 25 26

In New York City, nearly 800 languages are spoken! It's the most diverse city in the US.

HOW OONUH DA DO
20 6 15 15 26 19

The First Americans

There are more than 550 Indigenous American nations in the US, each with their own culture. These groups have lived in North America for thousands of years.

Fill in the crisscross grid with the names of each nation.

4 LETTERS
Hopi

5 LETTERS
Sioux Houma Kiowa

6 LETTERS
Apache Navajo Oglala

7 LETTERS
Tlingit Choctaw

8 LETTERS
Kickapoo Cherokee

10 LETTERS
Miccosukee

Write down all of the letters on the colored squares, then unscramble them to find the name of the state with the biggest proportion of Indigenous people.

Strange Stories

Lake monsters, swamp beasts, mysterious hairy apes... American culture is full of myths, legends, and strange stories about otherworldly creatures that have been passed from one generation to another.

Create a mythical creature or spooky ghost for your home town. First describe it, then draw it in the space below.

In Hawaiian legend, nightmarchers are ghosts of ancient warriors who rise from burial sites or the ocean to honor Hawaiian gods.

Bigfoot is a legendary ape-like creature said to live in the forests of northwestern US and Canada.

Name

Is it friendly or dangerous?

How big is it?

How does it move around?

Where does it live?

Now, use the space below to write a story about your creature or spirit.

Make it as funny, silly, or scary as you like!

Back in Time

How much do you know about American history? Historic sites and museums around the country teach visitors how the US has been shaped by people and events in the past.

Below are three people, three states, and three attractions. Can you work out who visited which attraction, and in which state? As you discover the answers, fill in the grid at the bottom of the page.

Felix

TENNESSEE

UNTO THESE HILLS
This play, performed every summer, tells the story of the Trail of Tears, when over 16,000 Cherokee people were forced out of their homelands.

Alia

MONTANA

BANNACK DAYS
This festival of pioneer life takes place at Bannack Ghost Town, which was founded during the largest gold rush outside of California.

Gabrielle

SOUTH CAROLINA

NATIONAL CIVIL RIGHTS MUSEUM
Built around the site of the assassination of Dr. Martin Luther King, Jr., this museum honors the history of the Civil Rights Movement.

CLUES:	NAME	STATE	ATTRACTION
The largest gold rush outside of California took place in Montana.			
Gabrielle visited a state bordering the ocean (use the map at the front of the book to help you).			
Neither Alia nor Gabrielle visited a museum.			

Odd Flag Out

Every US state and territory has its own flag. Even Washington, D.C., which isn't a state or a territory, has one!

Study the rows of flags below, and circle the one that matches the correct flag, shown on the left.

U.S. Virgin Islands

Mississippi

Washington, D.C.

Oklahoma

Alaska

Feeding the Nation

What did you eat for breakfast this morning?
Chances are it came from a farm somewhere in the US!

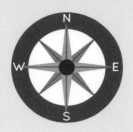

Each of these four farmers farms one of the crops or animals shown in the grid. Your job is to work out which. Follow the instructions given for each farmer to move them through the grid to the correct crop or animal. Use the compass to help you.

FARMER A

Move three squares east, two squares south, one square west.

I am farming

FARMER C

Move two squares west, three squares south, two squares northwest.

I am farming

FARMER B

Move three squares east, one square north, one square northeast.

I am farming

Mississippi has a higher percentage of Black farmers than any other state.

FARMER D

Move three squares west, two squares northeast, one square south.

I am farming

In Palmer, Alaska, some farmers harvest wool from musk oxen, huge creatures that used to live alongside saber-toothed tigers!

Time to Eat

People from all over the world live in the US,
bringing with them lots of tasty foods from different cultures.

Take a look at the seven foods below. Some of them
have been introduced from other countries,
while others were invented in the US.

Study them for 30 seconds, then turn the page and
write down as many as you can remember.

Pasta
(Italy)

Pretzel
(Germany)

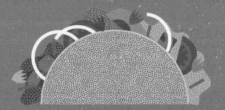

Taco
(Mexico)

Noodles
(China and other Asian countries)

Tex-Mex
(a mix of Mexican and Texan!)

Rice cakes
(songpyeon) (Korea)

Ice cream sundae
(invented in Wisconsin in 1881)

Write your answers to the **"Time to Eat"** memory challenge here.
How many did you manage to remember?

Sports Sudoku

From high school and college sports to national leagues, sports are an important part of American life. Do you have a favorite sport?

In this grid, draw one of these pieces of equipment in each square. Each row, column, and mini 4×4 grid must contain all four objects.

VOLLEYBALL **BASEBALL BAT**
FOOTBALL **STICKBALL STICK**

The islands of American Samoa raise more American football players than anywhere else in the world!

New Hampshire is the only state that offers ski jumping as a high school sport.

Stickball is a historic Choctaw game. It's one of the oldest organized sports in the US.

The Great Outdoors

Millions of Americans love to head outdoors to enjoy the incredible landscapes of the US, from vast deserts to snow-topped mountains.

This wordsearch contains the names of 12 fun outdoor activities. Can you find them all? The words might be written **forward**, **backward**, **up**, **down**, or **diagonally**.

1 Running

2 Fishing

3 Bridge jumping

One day a year, the state of West Virginia allows thrill-seekers to jump from the New River Bridge. It's nearly 900 feet tall!

12 Hiking

11 Bicycling

10 Surfing

9 Rock climbing

V	J	O	L	G	P	T	H	S	K	E	G	E	S
Z	H	H	R	I	N	I	P	A	T	D	N	G	C
Z	J	H	U	S	K	I	Y	R	G	Z	I	N	U
X	K	Q	N	I	L	A	L	G	M	O	F	I	B
X	S	V	N	W	K	V	G	C	B	E	R	D	A
X	C	G	I	I	L	Q	X	C	Y	V	U	R	D
B	P	P	N	R	U	V	P	I	P	C	S	A	I
R	A	G	G	N	I	H	S	I	F	X	I	O	V
G	N	I	H	C	T	A	W	D	R	I	B	B	I
F	P	B	Y	N	Q	W	F	A	M	H	V	W	N
R	P	W	D	Y	A	H	G	V	T	N	E	O	G
R	B	R	I	D	G	E	J	U	M	P	I	N	G
R	O	C	K	C	L	I	M	B	I	N	G	S	V
I	C	E	C	L	I	M	B	I	N	G	T	O	E

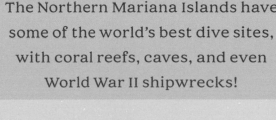

4 Ice climbing

The Northern Mariana Islands have some of the world's best dive sites, with coral reefs, caves, and even World War II shipwrecks!

5 Snowboarding

6 Birdwatching

7 Kayaking

8 Scuba diving

Off to Work

People in America work in all kinds of different jobs, from banking to beekeeping. What would you like to do when you grow up?

This fun quiz might help you decide! Just answer the questions and follow the arrows.

START HERE!
Do you prefer...

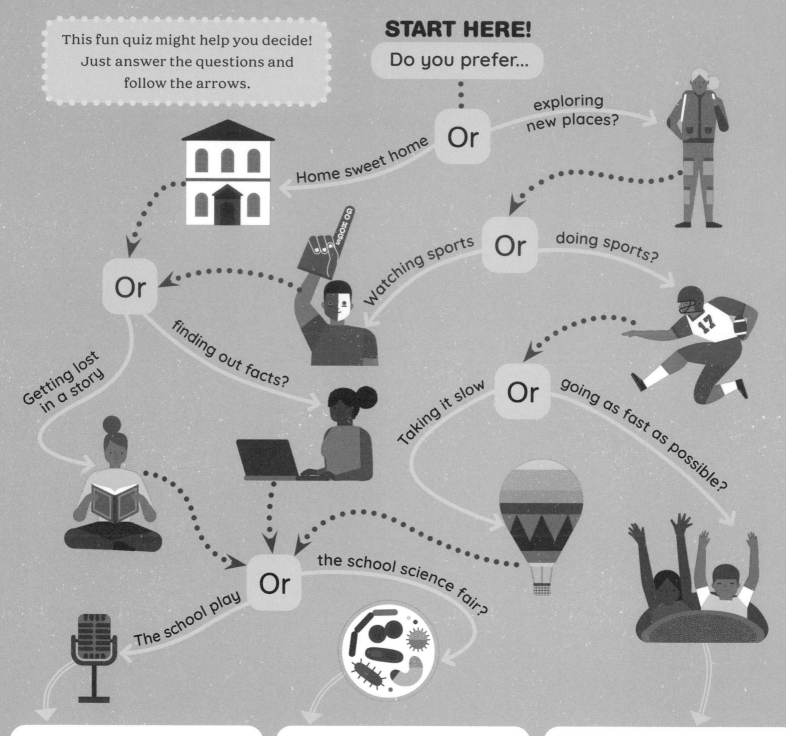

Home sweet home **Or** exploring new places?

Watching sports **Or** doing sports?

finding out facts? **Or** Getting lost in a story

Taking it slow **Or** going as fast as possible?

The school play **Or** the school science fair?

CREATIVE

You love being creative and using your imagination. Here are some jobs you might enjoy:

FILM-MAKER in Hollywood, California.

ARTIST in the creative arts hub of Santa Fe, New Mexico.

MUSICIAN in "Music City," also know as Nashville, Tennessee.

SCIENCE AND DISCOVERY

You like asking questions and finding out new things. You might like to try one of these jobs:

ROCKET SCIENTIST at the US Space & Rocket Center, Alabama.

FOSSIL SCIENTIST in Wyoming.

SPACE SCIENTIST searching for intelligent life in the universe at the Green Bank Telescope in West Virginia.

ACTION AND ADVENTURE

You like new challenges and being active! Maybe you could try one of these jobs:

COWBOY in Texas.

FORESTER in Georgia (there are over 54,000 working in the state!).

RANGER in Denali National Park, Alaska.

Cowboy Count Up

Cowboys are a famous symbol of the Wild West, and an important part of American culture. Today, people show off their cowboy skills at rodeos, and cowboys help to run large ranches.

Three cowboys are rounding up cattle. Work out how many cows each cowboy manages to rope, using the picture and the information below. Write the totals underneath each cowboy's name.

All three cowboys round up the **BROWN COWS**.
Leila ropes **2** more brown cows than Jackson, who ropes **3** more than Emma.
Leila and Jackson round up the **BLACK-AND-WHITE COWS**.
Leila ropes **TWICE** as many black-and-white cows as Jackson.

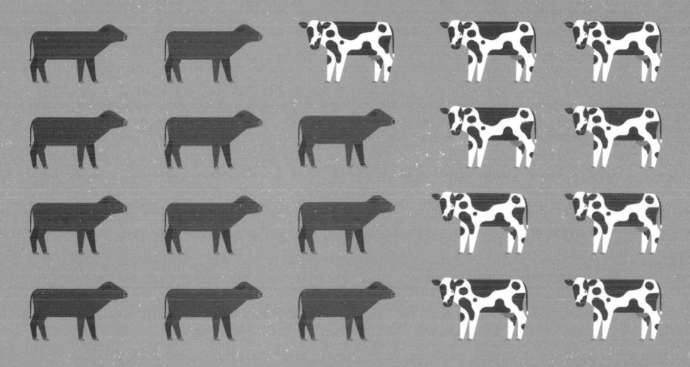

Leila

Jackson

Emma

_ _ _ _ _ _ brown cows

_ _ _ _ _ _ black-and-white cows

_ _ _ _ _ _ brown cows

_ _ _ _ _ _ black-and-white cows

_ _ _ _ _ _ brown cows

Space Maze

**MAE C. JEMISON
B. 1956**
The first Black woman
to travel into space.

On July 20, 1969, the US became the first nation to land a human on the Moon. Today, brainy people at NASA are working toward sending humans to the planet Mars. You might get to travel there someday!

**ALAN BARTLETT
SHEPARD JR
1923-1998**
The first American
to travel into space.

These four astronauts have been collecting rock samples on Mars. Can you help them each find their way back to their rocket?

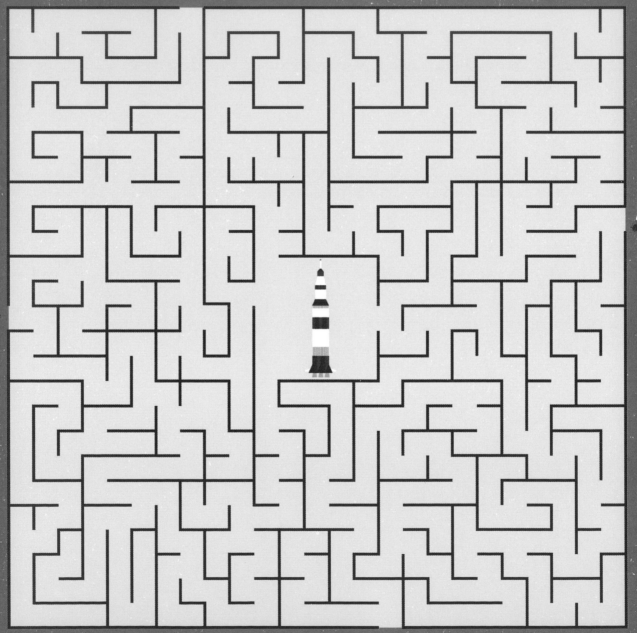

Imaginative Writers

The US has produced some of the greatest writers in the world.
Now it's time for you to show off your skill with words!

GWENDOLYN BROOKS

This famous poet and author was born in Kansas and grew up in Illinois.

How many words of three letters or more can you make from the letters in her name?

Edgar Allan Poe was born in Massachusetts. He wrote spooky, mysterious stories and poems. Write your own spine-chilling poem, where the first letter of the first word in each line spells "SPOOKY!"

S _____

P _____

O _____

O _____

K _____

Y _____

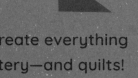

Creative Artists

Talented artists and craftspeople around the US create everything from paintings and sculptures to baskets and pottery—and quilts! Quiltmaking is a popular American hobby that goes back hundreds of years.

Design your own pattern on this quilt and color it in.

Most quilts are symmetrical: one half looks exactly like the other in reverse. If you'd like to make your quilt symmetrical, use the grid to help you. Design one square or section, then draw a mirror image of that design in the square or section opposite. Continue until you have a beautiful quilt!

Movie Magic

Some of the world's best movies are made in Hollywood, California—it's the biggest and oldest film industry in the world.

Now's your chance to create your own movie! A major Hollywood studio has just called and they want YOU to pitch an idea for a new action-adventure movie. Write your ideas below.

My movie is about

_____

_____

a tornado

an alien invasion

a swarm of killer bats

You can use one of the ideas here, or come up with your own.

My movie is set

_____

_____

in a waterpark

in space

on a school bus

Use one of the ideas here, or come up with your own.

My movie's hero is

_____

_____

_____

_____

_____

_____

_____

Describe them and give them a name.

This actor plays the hero

_____

(This could be someone famous, a friend, or you!)

This is how the hero saves the day

_____

_____

_____

_____

The name of my movie is

_____

RYAN COOGLER
B. 1986
Director of record-breaking, history-making movie *Black Panther*.

WALT DISNEY
1901–1966
Famous pioneer of animation.

American Inventions

Every time you switch on a light, use the Internet, or take a flight somewhere, you are using something invented in the United States! How much do you know about other American inventions?

Most of the facts on this page are true, but three have been made up—can you spot which? Read the statements, then circle the three fakes.

1. The first snowboard, invented in Michigan in 1965, was known as the "Snurfer."

2. The electric guitar was invented in Seattle, Washington, in 1732.

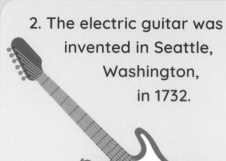

3. When basketball was invented by Massachusetts gym teacher James Naismith in 1891, he used peach baskets as goals.

4. One of the world's first computers, called ENIAC, was invented at the University of Pennsylvania in 1946. It weighed about the same as four school buses!

5. The original name for the Frisbee, invented by Walter Frederick Morrison in 1948, was the Pluto Platter.

6. The first Internet emoticon, invented by university professor Scott Fahlman in 1982, was a smiley face :-)

7. The steam train was invented in Dallas, Texas, in 1704.

8. Snow golf was invented in Vermont by *Jungle Book* author Rudyard Kipling.

9. The banana split was invented by President Thomas Jefferson in 1813 when he got bored of eating bananas on their own.

Inspiring Activists

Throughout US history, inspirational activists have fought for the rights of women, Indigenous Americans, Black people, and many other groups, and also brought attention to important issues such as climate change.

Design a protest poster about something you care about.

SOJOURNER TRUTH
c. 1797–1883

A formerly enslaved person who fought for abolition, and civil and women's rights.

NINA E. ALLENDER
1873–1957

Argued for women's rights at a time when women were not allowed to vote.

DOROTHEA LYNDE DIX
1802–1887

Stood up for the rights of people with mental illnesses.

Innovative Scientists

Millions of Americans work as scientists in the US. New Jersey has more engineers and scientists per square mile than anywhere else in world!

There are many different types of scientists. Can you draw lines to match each job title with the correct job description?

Marine biologist

Paleontologist

Chemist

Epidemiologist

Astronomer

Zoologist

Meteorologist

Physicist

 Studies the causes and patterns of diseases in humans.

 Studies the fossils of animals and plants that lived millions of years ago.

 Studies life in the ocean.

 Studies space—the Sun, Moon, stars, planets, and other objects.

 Studies how animals behave.

 Studies the day-to-day weather.

 Studies matter (the stuff everything is made of) and energy.

 Studies chemicals and how they react with each other.

Which type of scientist would you most like to be?

Supercomputer Solutions

Powerful supercomputers can solve all types of problems. Some can perform quadrillions of calculations in a second! How quick are YOU at calculating? Let's find out!

Find a way though these number mazes from left to right, adding up the numbers as you go, so that you end up with the number above each maze. Only one route will give you the correct total, and each number can only be used once. You may go **left**, **right**, **up**, or **down**, but not diagonally.

Make 12

2	1	4
7	6	8
9	2	1

Start → ... End

Here is an example.

Make 15

3	4	5
4	6	2
8	2	1

Start → ... End

Make 20

2	1	9
3	2	3
4	9	4

Start → ... End

Make 26

5	7	9	1
2	6	3	2
4	1	8	1

Start → ... End

Make 47

12	5	6	1
3	4	11	5
5	6	1	2

Start → ... End

DOROTHY VAUGHAN
1910–2008
Mathematician, computer programmer, and the first Black woman to manage an entire divison of NASA.

Music Makers

Jazz, blues, gospel, rock 'n' roll, electronic dance music, and hip-hop all started in the US, and Nashville, Tennessee, is the country music capital of the world!

Draw lines from each of these silhouettes of musicians to the matching picture at the bottom of the page.

Sweet Treats

The US may be known for its fresh fruit and vegetables, but anyone with a sweet tooth knows it's also the place to go for a yummy snack.

Each of these treats costs a different amount: **$1, $2, $3, $4**, or **$5**. Using the sums below, can you work out the price of each one?

Providence, Rhode Island has more doughnut shops per person than anywhere else in the country.

Doughnut	Snowball	Popcorn	Soda	Ice cream cone
$ _____	$ _____	$ _____	$ _____	$ _____

Let's Celebrate!

The US is a kaleidoscope of different cultures and communities.
This diversity is celebrated in colorful festivals around the country,
where people can enjoy food, music, dancing, and parades.

Czech festival Wilbur, Nebraska	**Prince Lot Hula Festival** Hawaii	**Thai New Year** Los Angeles, California	**St Patrick's Day Parade** New York City, New York
	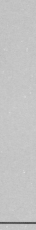		
Guam Micronesia Island Fair Guam	**Gathering of Nations** Albuquerque, New Mexico	**West Indian Day Parade** New York City, New York	**Odunde Festival** Philadelphia, Pennsylvania

Italian Festival Memphis, Tennessee	**Norsk Festival** Minot, North Dakota	**Calle Ocho festival** Little Havana district, Miami, Florida	**Teuila Festival** American Samoa

These two pages show some of these festivals. Can you spot the differences between the pictures on the left page and right page?

There is **one** difference per picture.

A celebration of Czech culture in the US's Czech capital.	The largest hula event in Hawaii, showcasing island culture.	A celebration by the largest Thai population outside of Thailand.	The world's largest and oldest Irish parade.

People from Micronesia come together to celebrate their islands' unique traditions.	North America's largest powwow, or gathering, of Indigenous peoples.	This celebration of Caribbean American communities is one of the largest parades in North America.	Up to 500,000 people gather to celebrate African, Caribbean, and Black culture.
	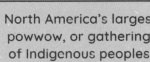		
A celebration of Italian culture that includes traditions like grape-stomping.	Many North Dakotans acknowledge their Scandinavian roots at this annual celebration.	Florida's biggest Hispanic festival.	An annual celebration of Samoan and Polynesian culture.

Explore the US

It's time to take a final trip around the US! As you hop from state to state, you'll join in with regional traditions, festivals, and events. The more of the US you experience, the better your chance of winning the game!

To play, you'll need **another player**, **a die**, and **two game pieces**—these can be anything small, like coins or buttons. Take turns to roll the die and move your game piece, following any instructions on the circle you land on. The winner is the first player to visit six different states AND reach the finish line.

START!
Roll the die to begin.

Spend a few fun days hanging out with cowboys at a Dude Ranch in WYOMING.

MISS A GO

Race with the world's best jockeys at the KENTUCKY Derby, America's biggest horse race. Disaster—your horse bolts!

**Roll the die:
if you roll 1-3, your horse gallops FORWARD 1 SPACE.
If you roll 4-6, it gallops BACK 1 SPACE.**

Duck to avoid dried cow poop being hurled at the World Cow Chip Throwing Contest in OKLAHOMA.

RUN BACK 3 SPACES, QUICKLY!

Stop to watch some of the greatest racecar drivers at the famous Indy 500 race, in INDIANA—and get a lift from the winner!

SPEED FORWARD 3 SPACES

It's the Strolling of the Heifers parade in VERMONT. All those cows are blocking the street!

MISS A GO

Enter the Emma Crawford Coffin Races, one of the most unique traditions in COLORADO.

RACE FORWARD 1 SPACE

Hitch an RV ride heading to sunny ARIZONA for the winter.

CRUISE FORWARD 1 SPACE

Enter the iconic Ironman triathlon in HAWAII. It's a 112-mile bike ride, 26-mile run, and 2-mile swim...

MISS A GO WHILE YOU RECOVER

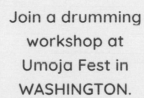

Help out on the floating post office that delivers mail to ships on the Detroit River in MICHIGAN.

FLOAT FORWARD 2 SPACES

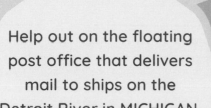

Join a drumming workshop at Umoja Fest in WASHINGTON.

MISS A GO

Hop aboard for the century-old tradition of lobster boat racing in MAINE.

CHUG FORWARD 1 SPACE

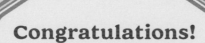

Congratulations!

You've completed your trip around the US!
Have you visited six states? If not, go back to the start and keep on counting.

Enter the Rolling in the Grits contest at the World Grits Festival in SOUTH CAROLINA. Now you're covered in grits!

GO BACK TO THE START TO GET CLEANED UP

ANSWERS

WHO'S WHO?

Marie Z. Chino

SAY HELLO!

Navajo
Spanish
Hawaiian
Arabic
Hindi
Yoruba (spoken in West Africa)
Gullah (spoken in some African American communities in coastal South Carolina and Georgia)

THE FIRST AMERICANS

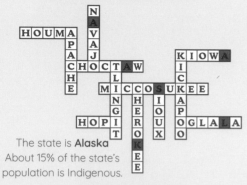

The state is **Alaska**
About 15% of the state's population is Indigenous.

BACK IN TIME

NAME	STATE	ATTRACTION
Alia	Montana	Bannack Days
Gabrielle	South Carolina	Unto These Hills
Felix	Tennessee	National Civil Rights Museum

ODD FLAG OUT

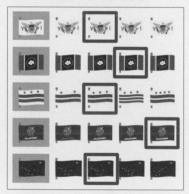

FEEDING THE NATION

A—pumpkins; B—mushrooms;
C—chickens; D—corn

SPORTS SUDOKU

THE GREAT OUTDOORS

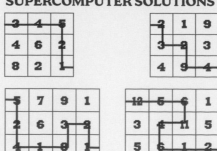

COWBOY COUNT UP

Leila—6 brown cows,
6 black-and-white cows
Jackson—4 brown cows,
3 black-and-white cows
Emma—1 brown cow

SPACE MAZE

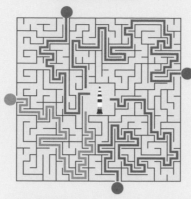

AMERICAN INVENTIONS

2. FALSE—The electric guitar was actually invented in 1932. Electricity hadn't even been discovered in 1732!

7. FALSE—The steam train was invented a hundred years later in the United Kingdom. In 1704, Dallas didn't even exist.

9. FALSE—The banana split was invented in the US, but in 1904 and not by President Thomas Jefferson.

INNOVATIVE SCIENTISTS

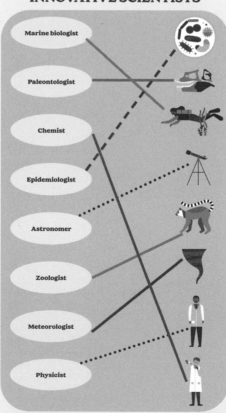

Marine biologist
Paleontologist
Chemist
Epidemiologist
Astronomer
Zoologist
Meteorologist
Physicist

SUPERCOMPUTER SOLUTIONS

MUSIC MAKERS

SWEET TREATS

Doughnut—**$1**; Snowball—**$2**; Popcorn—**$4**;
Soda—**$3**; Ice cream cone—**$5**

LET'S CELEBRATE!

Q The Quarto Group
Inspiring | Educating | Creating | Entertaining

Brimming with creative inspiration, how-to projects, and useful information to enrich your everyday life, quarto.com is a favorite destination for those pursuing their interests and passions.

We Are the United States Activity Book © 2023 Quarto Publishing plc.
Text © 2023 Quarto Publishing plc.
Illustrations © 2022 Sol Linero.
Text reproduced from *We Are the United States* © 2022 Sarosh Arif and Margeaux Weston.
Based on the book *We Are the United States* by Sarosh Arif, Margeaux Weston, and Sol Linero.

First published in 2023 by Wide Eyed Editions, an imprint of the Quarto Group.
100 Cummings Center, Suite 265D,
Beverly, MA 01915, US.
T (978) 282-9590 F (978) 283-2742

1 Triptych Place
London, SE1 9SH, UK.
T (0)20 7700 6700 F (0)20 7700 8066
WTS TAX d.o.o., Žanova ulica 3, 4000 Kranj, Slovenia.
www.wts-tax.si
www.Quarto.com

ISBN 978-0-7112-8263-6

Written by Claire Saunders • Designed by Lyli Feng
Edited by Alex Hithersay • Published by Debbie Foy

Manufactured in Guangzhou, China EB122022

9 8 7 6 5 4 3 2 1

MIX
Paper from responsible sources
FSC® C124385